PAST IN PICTURES

A photographic view of
World War One

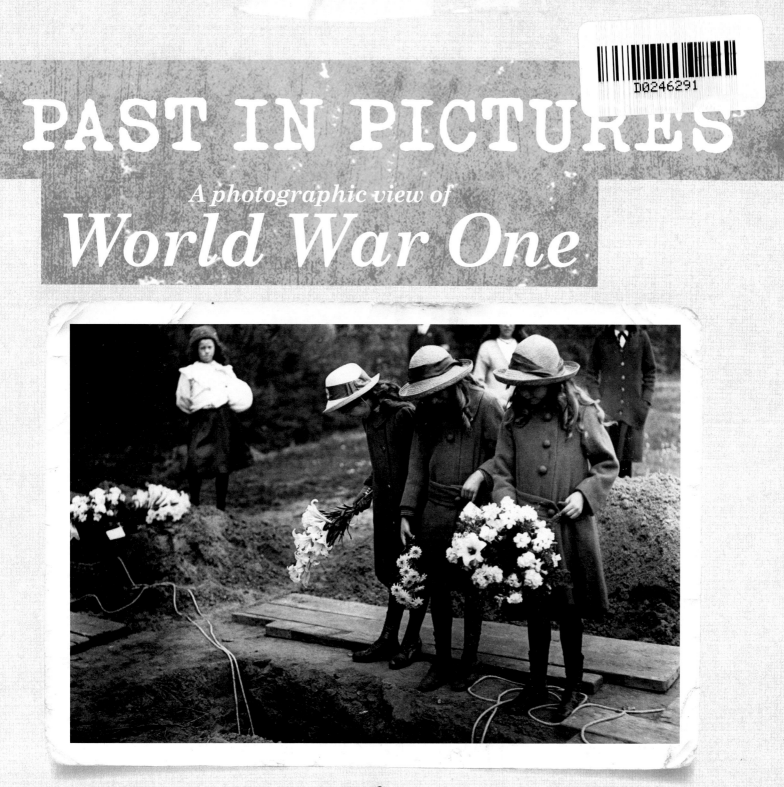

Published in paperback in 2014 by Wayland
Copyright © Wayland 2014

Wayland
338 Euston Road
London NW1 3BH

Wayland Australia
Level 17/207 Kent Street
Sydney, NSW 2000

Editor: Joyce Bentley
Concept Design: Lisa Peacock
Designer: Elaine Wilkinson
Researchers: Laura Simpson and Hester Vaizey at
The National Archives

Picture acknowledgements:
Material reproduced by courtesy of The
National Archives, London, England. www.
nationalarchives.gov.uk. Catalogue references and
picture acknowledgements Main cover: Hulton-
Deutsch Collection/CORBIS (tl); MUN4-1085 Gun
Ammunition (5) 1916 (tr); FO383-413 (4) French
and British POWs arrive at camp from the front,
World War I, 1918 (bl); EXT1-315 Pt2 Women Come
And Help poster WWI (br); Back cover: NATS1-
1308 God Speed The Plough And The Woman Who
Drives It 1917 (l); MUN5-165-1124-49 Keighley
National Shell Factory 1915 (r); title page: Hulton-
Deutsch Collection/CORBIS; p2: MUN4-1085 Gun
Ammunition (5) 1916; p3: Getty Images; p4: ADM1-
8331 The Navy Wants Men poster WWI; p5: Hulton-
Deutsch Collection/CORBIS; p6: MUN4-1085 Gun
Ammunition (5) 1916; p7: EXT1-315 The Big Push
poster; p8: EXT1-315 1 of 2 German trenches before
bombardment, EXT1-315 2 of 2 German trenches
after bombardment; p9: EXT1-315 Learn To Make
Munitions poster; p10: MUN5-165-1124-49 Keighley
National Shell Factory 1915; p11: p.11: NATS 1-109
War Work Enrol Today Release A Fit Man For The
Front 1914-1918; p12: EXT1-315 Pt2 Women Come
And Help poster WWI; p13: MAF59-3 Womens' Land
Army girl with horse-drawn harrow; p14: NATS1-
1308 God Speed The Plough And The Woman Who
Drives It 1917; p15: MAF42-8 Womens' Land Army
armlet 1917-1918 (t), MAF42-8 Womens' Land Army
certificate (b); p16: NATS 1-1308 Women's Land
Army booklet. Join The Land Army 1917; p17: Getty
Images; p18: Getty Images; p19: AIR1-569-16-15-142
House interior after an air raid on Hull, 6-7 June
1915; p20: Getty Images; p21: NSC7-37 Food Control
Campaign Adopt Voluntary Rations 1916-1917; p22:
Getty Images; p23: FO383-413 (4) French and British
POWs arrive at camp from the front, World War I,
1918; p24: RAIL 253-516 Postcard message from
Jack Symons 27 September 1915 (t), RAIL253-516
Sgt Jack Symons KRR 1915 (b); p25: WO339-51440
Siegfried Sassoon concern over state of mental health
1918; p26: Mary Evans Picture Library/Pump Park
Photography; p27: Mary Evans Picture Library/Pump
Park Photography; p28: WO138-74 Lieut Wilfred E
S Owen killed in action 1918; p29: Hulton-Deutsch
Collection/CORBIS

A cataloguing record for this title is available at the
British Library.

Dewey number: 940.4'00222-dc23

ISBN: 978 0 7502 8339 7

Printed in China

10 9 8 7 6 5 4 3 2 1

Wayland is a division of Hachette Children's Books,
an Hachette UK company
www.hachette.co.uk

Contents

Introduction

In this book we look at photographs and other kinds of images from World War One. We examine these images for clues about the conflict, and see what we can learn from them about how people's lives were affected by the war. On pages 30-31, you can find some questions and points to explore, to encourage further discussion of the pictures.

Recruitment

THE NAVY WANTS MEN

Recruits required at once for

R.N.V.R.
SIGNAL BRANCH
INCLUDING WIRELESS TELEGRAPHY.

QUALIFICATIONS

AGE: 17 years and 6 months to 22 years.
EDUCATION: Not below ex-seventh standard, Good Writing and Spelling. Good Eyesight and Hearing.

PAY FROM 1/3 A DAY
And Separation Allowance.

APPLY:
Naval Recruiting Office,
Great Scotland Yard, S.W. 1.

← This poster is encouraging men to join the Royal Navy.

← During World War I, many thousands of young men joined the armed forces in order to fight. They were persuaded partly by posters such as this one. War broke out on 4 August 1914. By 5 September, more than 225,000 men had volunteered.

↓ Young men queue up to join the army.

↑ For the first six months, the war was popular and men were eager to sign up to fight. Then, as reports came back of the terrible conditions at the front, recruitment levels fell. In January 1916, the government introduced conscription, which meant that most single men between the ages of 18 and 41 were forced to join the armed forces.

Munitions

⬇ In this factory they are making explosive shells to fire at the enemy.

↑ Munitions factories in World War I could be dangerous places. Workers were exposed to harmful chemicals with little or no protection. Because the army needed munitions quickly, safety was often ignored. In January 1917, 73 people were killed or injured in an explosion at a London munitions factory.

→ This poster is urging munitions workers not to take holidays.

→ By 1915, there was a major shortage of artillery shells on the front lines. A law was passed to stop people from leaving their jobs in the factories. To increase production rates, munitions workers were encouraged not to take holidays.

Reproduced by the Special Permission of the Proprietors of "Punch."

THE BIG PUSH.

MUNITION WORKER. "WELL, I'M NOT TAKING A HOLIDAY MYSELF JUST YET, BUT I'M SENDING THESE KIDS OF MINE FOR A LITTLE TRIP ON THE CONTINENT."

GERMAN TRENCHES
On the WESTERN FRONT.
(1) BEFORE BOMBARDMENT.

KX 481

⬇ These photos show the effects of bombing on the German trenches.

↑ Great efforts were made to make factory workers feel part of the war effort, even if they weren't actually fighting. These posters are reminding workers that the bombs they are making will do great damage to the enemy.

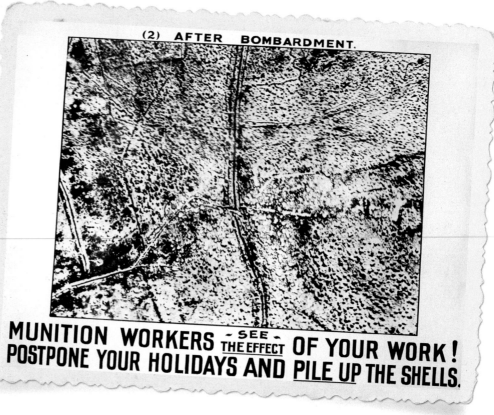

(2) AFTER BOMBARDMENT.

MUNITION WORKERS - SEE - THE EFFECT OF YOUR WORK!
POSTPONE YOUR HOLIDAYS AND PILE UP THE SHELLS.

→ Women were urged to go and work in munitions factories.

→ Because of the shell shortage, and because so many men were away fighting, munitions factories began employing women for the first time. By the end of the war, there were almost a million 'munitionettes' producing weapons and ammunition for the British army.

THESE WOMEN ARE DOING THEIR BIT

LEARN TO MAKE MUNITIONS

> → Women in munitions factories worked very hard for little pay.

↑ Munitionettes worked with dangerous chemicals without proper protection. Prolonged exposure to sulphur turned their skin yellow. Some were killed in factory explosions. On average, women were paid less than half of what men were paid for doing the same job.

→ This poster is asking people to do war work.

→ During World War I, German U-boats (submarines) sank many ships carrying food and other supplies to Britain, causing severe shortages. This poster uses a violent image to emphasise the seriousness of the crisis Britain faced. It calls on people who are not eligible to fight, such as women or older men, to enrol for war work, so that fit young men working in the factories can go to the front.

← Women are being asked to help to build aircraft.

← Aeroplanes had only recently been invented when World War I broke out. At first they were used to spy on the enemy. Later, they were used to fight other aircraft and to drop bombs. By 1918, there were nearly 350,000 workers, many of them women, employed building aircraft in Britain.

→ This woman is working for the Women's Land Army.

→ The Women's Land Army (WLA) was founded during World War I. The WLA arranged for women to work as farm labourers to replace the men who had been called up to fight. The women who worked for the WLA were popularly known as land girls.

← A recruitment poster for the Women's Land Army.

← The Women's Land Army was set up in 1915. By the end of 1917, there were around 20,000 land girls working on British farms. They worked 50 hours a week – longer during harvest time – with only Saturday afternoons and Sundays off.

→ The arm band worn by members of the Women's Land Army.

Every woman who helps in agriculture during the war is as truly serving her country as the man who is fighting in the trenches or on the sea.

Walter Runciman
President of the Board of Trade.

Selborne
President of the Board of Agriculture.

← A certificate awarded to women on achieving entry to the Women's Land Army.

← The land girls were paid £1 per week (about £65 in today's money) and received free work clothing and accommodation in local hostels. Work uniforms included trousers – quite a shocking change in women's clothing!

⬇ Leaflets like this one persuaded many women to join the WLA.

W 17

Join
the
Land Army

A Call to the
Women of
Great Britain

WOMEN of Great Britain, an appeal has never yet been made to you in vain.

You have flocked into the Hospitals and Munition Factories; large numbers of you have gone on to the land; you have undertaken every kind of voluntary service. You have shown the same patriotic and fervent spirit as the men, and the War cannot be brought to a victorious end without you.

⬆ Although some farmers were initially resistant to the idea of the WLA, most women proved to be very able farm workers. 'Good service' stripes were awarded after six months of satisfactory work. The war ended in 1918, but the WLA continued until 1919, when the men returned from the armed forces. Some land girls stayed on after that as permanent workers.

Refugees

↓ These refugees from Belgium are staying in a workhouse in London.

↑ At the start of the war, more than 250,000 refugees arrived in Britain from Belgium. It was the largest refugee movement in British history. They were housed in hostels and other accommodation around the country. Most returned to Belgium when the war ended.

↓ This shop has been damaged by German shelling.

↑ Merryweather's, a shop in Scarborough, Yorkshire, was badly hit during a bombardment by German warships in December 1914. This was one of a series of German raids on Britain's east coast during World War I. Other raids struck Hartlepool, Whitby, Yarmouth and Lowestoft.

↓ A couple look at the damage to their house after an air raid.

↑ This house in Hull was damaged during a Zeppelin raid in June 1915. Zeppelins were German airships used to bomb British cities in World War I. Early raids caused lots of casualties but by 1916, British defences improved and many Zeppelins were shot down. The Zeppelin campaign was called off in 1917.

Food shortages and rationing

↓ A boy and his father dig up potatoes on an allotment.

↑ Because the German U-boat campaign (see page 11) caused food shortages in Britain, food prices rose. As a result, many people began to grow their own food in their gardens and on allotments,like this one in Dulwich, London.

→ This poster is encouraging people to eat a little less because of food shortages.

→ In 1916, the government introduced 'voluntary rationing' – people were encouraged to limit their food intake. This did not work, and many poor people began to starve. In 1918, rationing was imposed. People could only buy limited amounts of sugar, meat, butter and cheese.

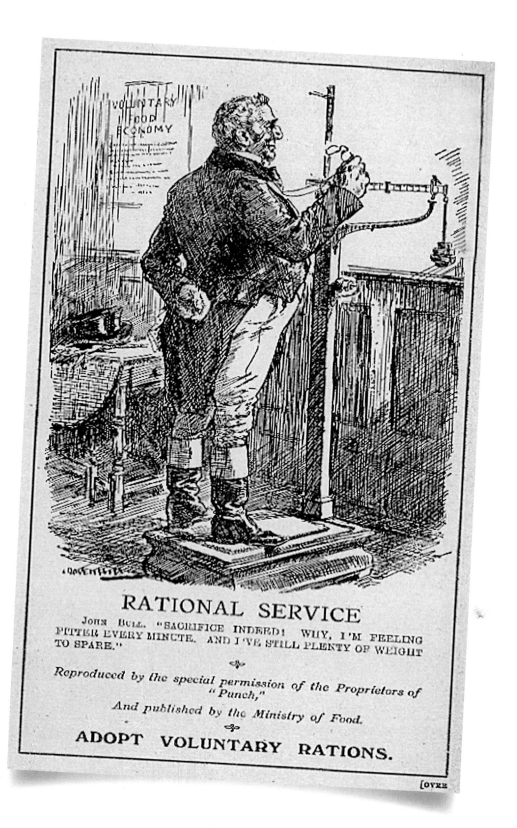

RATIONAL SERVICE

JOHN BULL. "SACRIFICE INDEED! WHY, I'M FEELING FITTER EVERY MINUTE. AND I'VE STILL PLENTY OF WEIGHT TO SPARE."

Reproduced by the special permission of the Proprietors of "Punch,"

And published by the Ministry of Food.

ADOPT VOLUNTARY RATIONS.

Anti-German sentiment

↓ People gather to protest outside a German shop in London.

↑ During World War I, many British people felt angry towards Germany and there were several anti-German riots. Suspected Germans were assaulted and stores with German-sounding names were attacked. Even King George V was persuaded to change his German family name of Saxe-Coburg and Gotha to Windsor.

Prisoners of war

↓ British and French prisoners of war arrive at a German prison camp.

↑ During World War I, around eight million men surrendered and became prisoners of war (POWs). They were held in POW camps until the war ended. International rules on the treatment of prisoners were agreed. However, many prisoners were treated harshly.

NOTHING is to be written on this side except the date and signature of the sender. Sentences not required may be erased. If anything else is added the post card will be destroyed.

I am quite well.

~~I have been admitted into hospital~~

{ ~~sick~~ } ~~and am going on well.~~
{ ~~wounded~~ } ~~and hope to be discharged soon.~~

~~I am being sent down to the ba~~

~~I have received your~~ { ~~letter d~~
{ ~~telegra~~
{ ~~parcel~~

Letter follows at first opport

~~I have received no letter from~~

{ ~~lately.~~
{ ~~for a long time.~~

Signature }
only. } *Jack S*

27.9

Date _____

[Postage must be prepaid on
addressed to the send

(25540) Wt. W3497-293 1,000m. 8/15 M

↓ Here we can see a photograph and a postcard sent from a soldier to his family.

↑ There were strict rules regarding what soldiers could say in letters and postcards home. They were not allowed to say where they were, in case the correspondence fell into enemy hands. They were also barred from making any negative comments about the war as the authorities feared this would damage morale on the home front.

→ This letter is expressing concern about the mental health of a soldier.

→ Many men who fought in the trenches suffered from 'shell shock' – mental breakdown due to prolonged exposure to enemy bombardment. Siegfried Sassoon was an officer decorated for bravery. He was also a poet who described the horrors of the trenches in detail. The authorities decided to send him to be treated for shell shock.

122091/5 (M.I.7.)

Personal & Confidential   20th. July, 1918.

Dear Sir,

Attention has been drawn to some verses on p. 394 of your issue of the 13th. July, 1918, signed by Siegfried Sassoon. Presumably, therefore, the author is Captain S. L. Sassoon, M.C., of the 3rd. Bn. Royal Welsh Fusiliers.

This Officer in July 1917, was reported by a medical board to be suffering from a nervous breakdown and not responsible for his actions, but at the end of November, 1917, he was found to have recovered and to be fit for General Service. He is now serving in France.

Your Reviewer on p. 400 of the same issue recognises clearly what was the state of Mr. Sassoon's mind when he wrote "Counter-attack and other Poems", but if Capt. Sassoon were now writing verse such as that printed on p. 394, it would appear that his mind is still chaos, and that he is not fit to be trusted with mens' lives. I should therefore be grateful if you would let me know when you received his verses "I stood with the dead". It may be, of course, that they have been in your possession some months. The information, which is desired solely in the public interest, will of course be treated as confidential.

Yours faithfully,

(sgd) George Cockerill

Brig- General
D. D. M. I.

A. W. Massingham. Esq.
The Editor,
"The Nation".

25

↓ Two British soldiers stand in a flooded trench on the Western Front.

↑ During World War I, a vast network of heavily defended trenches marked the front line. For soldiers in these trenches, death from enemy shelling or sniper fire was a constant danger. Conditions could be atrocious, as trenches were often infested with rats and lice. When it rained, trenches quickly became filled with muddy water which could cause trench walls to collapse. The water also attracted scores of frogs, slugs and beetles. Trench foot was a fungal infection caused by standing in wet trenches, and could result in amputation.

⬇ British soldiers keep warm around an oven on the Western Front.

↑ At breakfast time, the soldiers on either side of the front line would sometimes observe an unofficial truce – they would stop firing at each other while the meal was served and eaten. Often, the wagons bringing in food were not fired upon either. These truces rarely lasted long, however: if a senior officer heard about one, he would quickly put a stop to it.

← This is an official report of the death of a soldier.

FIELD SERVICE.

REPORT of Death of an Officer to be forwarded to the War Office with the least possible delay after receipt of notification of death on Army Form B. 213 or Army Form A. 36 or from other official documentary sources.

REGIMENT or CORPS	2nd Bn MANCHESTER REGT.	Squadron, Troop, Battery or Company

Rank	2/Lt.	
Name	OWEN, W.E.S.	
	By whom reported	O.C. Bn. 25/11/18.
	Date of Death	4/11/18.
DIED	Place or Hospital	France.
	Cause of Death	Killed in Action.
	Place of Burial	------

State whether he leaves a will or not — Not received.

All private documents and effects received from the front or hospital, should be examined, and if any will is found it should be at once forwarded to the War Office.

Not received.

Any information received as to verbal expressions by a deceased Officer of his wishes as to the disposal of his estate should be reported to the War Office as soon as possible.

Not received.

Signature of Officer in charge of Section Adjutant General's Office at the Base.
L R Chapman

Capt., for Officer i/c Infantry Section, No. 6, G.H.Q., 3rd Echelon, B.E.F.

Station and Date 11/11/18.

← World War I was one of the deadliest conflicts in history, with around 10 million military deaths. British military losses totalled 673,375. After the death of a soldier, reports like this one were sent to the War Office and then letters were sent out informing their next of kin.

↓ Girls stand over the grave of a victim of an air raid.

↑ About six million civilians, from throughout Europe, died in World War I. In Britain, 2,231 civilians lost their lives from air and sea bombardment or in U-boat attacks. However, most of the focus was on deaths at the front. War memorials were built in towns across the country. Every year on 11 November – Remembrance Day – people remember all those who fought and died for their country in World War I.

Questions to Ask and Points to Explore

Picture on page 4
Questions to ask
1. Where are these men, and what is the man with the telescope doing?
2. Do you think this poster would have been effective in persuading men to join the Navy? Would it be effective today?
3. Look at the list of qualifications. Why do you think the Navy wants men with those abilities?

Points to explore
Design: artwork, typography, effectiveness
Text: meaning of terms; old money
Content: age, gender and uniforms of people; flags

Photograph on page 5
Questions to ask
1. Why do you think the people queuing up look so happy?
2. At what point in the war do you think this photo was taken?

Points to explore
Background: style of building; sign
People: gender, age, clothing, hats

Photograph on page 6
Questions to ask
1. What do you think these men are making here?
2. Under the Munitions of War Act munitions workers were not allowed to leave their jobs without their employer's permission. Why do you think the government passed this law?

Points to explore
Background: machinery, exposed girders and wiring, metal shavings
People: gender, age, clothing, hat, hairstyles

Picture on page 7
Questions to ask
1. Do you know what is meant by the phrase 'the big push'? Do some research on trench warfare and see if you can find out.
2. What does the phrase: 'I'm sending these kids of mine for a little trip on the continent' mean? What does this tell us about attitudes towards war during this period?

Points to explore
Design: artwork, typography, effectiveness
Content: faces drawn on shells; worker's clothing and gender

Photographs on page 8
Questions to ask
1. Why do you think the government wanted to show these photos to munitions workers?
2. How can you tell that the photos show the same piece of landscape?

Points to explore
Design: layout and typography; use of capital letters and exclamation mark
Text: simplicity of language and message
Photos: roads; trenches; shell craters

Picture on page 9
Questions to ask
1. Do you think this poster would have been effective in encouraging women to go and work in factories? Give reasons why.
2. What does 'These women are doing their bit' mean?
3. Why is there a soldier in this illustration?

Points to explore
Design: artwork, layout and typography
Content: age, gender, clothing

Photograph on page 10
Questions to ask
1. There are some men in suits and ties on the factory floor. What do you think they are doing there?
2. Why do you think the women working on the machines had to wear caps?

Points to explore
Background: size of factory floor; machinery; trolleys; raw materials
People: gender; clothing; age

Picture on page 11
Questions to ask
1. What is meant by 'Germany means to starve us out'?
2. What is meant by 'Enrol today and release a fit man for the front'?

Points to explore
Design: effectiveness of typography and artwork
Content: What do the three characters represent? Why is the boy carrying a basket of food?

Photograph on page 12
Questions to ask
1. The aeroplanes in the poster have two pairs of wings, one above the other. Do you know what this type of plane is called?
2. How does this poster make the job of building aircraft seem more glamorous than it probably is?

Points to explore
Design: effectiveness of layout, typography and artwork style
Content: gender, age and clothing of woman; type of aircraft

Picture on page 13
Questions to ask
1. This land girl is using a harrow – a piece of equipment that is dragged over land to break up clods and remove weeds. Why do you think the harrow is being pulled by a horse and not a tractor?
2. In what way are the wheels of the harrow different from those you might find on modern farm vehicles?

Points to explore
Background: field; building; equipment; horse
Person: age, clothing, hat

Picture on page 14
Questions to ask
1. Do you think this poster would attract women to the idea of joining the WLA? In what ways is it effective?
2. 'God speed the plough' comes from a ploughman's song. Can you think of any other phrases you might use on a WLA recruiting poster? Think about how you might encourage a young woman from the city to become a farm labourer.

Points to explore
Design: effectiveness of artwork, typography and layout
Content: horse-drawn plough; woman's clothing; rural landscape; birds; stylised sun

Picture on page 15
Questions to ask
1. Why might wearing an arm band and being awarded a certificate make women feel proud to serve in the Women's Land Army?
2. How does the design of this certificate give the impression that it carries high status?

Points to explore
Armband: emblem
Certificate: coat of arms; text; signatures
Design: effectiveness of artwork, typography and layout

Picture on page 16
Questions to ask
1. Read the text of this leaflet. Do you find the writing persuasive? What techniques have the writers used to persuade readers to join the WLA? Look up 'patriotic' in the dictionary, then write a sentence using it.
Points to explore
Design: typography and layout

Photograph on page 17
Questions to ask
1. Do some research on workhouses. What would it have been like to live in one?
2. Why do you think the boy is waving a flag?
Points to explore
Background: building; windows; courtyard, flag; gramophone
People: ages; gender; clothing

Photograph on page 18
Questions to ask
1. The man on the right in the apron is probably the shopkeeper. Imagine you are him and write a short letter to a friend describing the raid and its effect on your business.
2. The raid began around 8 o'clock the morning and lasted for 30 minutes. Seventeen people were killed and 800 injured. What do you think life would have been like for residents during the raid and in the weeks that followed?
Points to explore
Background: building; damage; rubble
People: age; clothing

Photograph on page 19
Questions to ask
1. World War I was the first 'total war', where civilians found themselves in the line of fire. How did technology bring this about?
2. Think of five words to describe the feelings of the couple in this photograph.
Points to explore
Building: damaged walls; exposed ceiling joists
People: emotions; clothing

Photograph on page 20
Questions to ask
1. When war first broke out, there was panic-buying and shops sold out of food in days. Why do you think this happened?
2. During World War I, people had to eat whatever could be grown or reared in this country. List some of the foods you've eaten this week. How many of these would not have been available in World War I?

Points to explore
Background: allotment
People: age; gender; clothing

Picture on page 21
Questions to ask
1. Why do you think the voluntary code of rationing did not work?
2. Who is John Bull? What is he standing on?
3. 'Rational service' is a play on words. Can you see the terms being combined here?
Points to explore
Design: artwork; layout; typography
Content: John Bull's clothing and weight

Photograph on page 22
Questions to ask
1. This photograph was taken in June 1915, shortly after a riot against a German-owned shop in London. Can you see which shop was the target of the crowd's anger? Why do you think they attacked that shop?
2. How would you feel if you were a German living in London during World War I?
Points to explore
Background: buildings; damage; shop sign
People: ages, genders; clothing

Photograph on page 23
Questions to ask
Many POWs in Germany suffered from malnutrition and were kept in crowded, unhygienic conditions. However, they were relieved to be away from the front line. Imagine you are a POW in a German camp. Write a letter home describing your feelings and experiences.
Points to explore
Background: prison camp buildings
People: numbers; mood; gender; uniforms

Picture on page 24
Questions to ask
1. Do you think the authorities are right to be so careful about what soldiers can and can't say in their letters and postcards?
Points to explore
Photograph side: age, gender and uniforms of soldiers; rural scenery – no identifiable buildings
Writing side: warning at the top; preprinted text

Photograph on page 25
Questions to ask
1. In this letter, Sassoon is described as having had a 'nervous breakdown'. Why do you think the letter writer decided to describe him in this way? Read Sassoon's poems 'Counter-attack' and 'I Stood With the Dead'. Why might these poems worry the authorities?

Points to explore
Text: overall purpose of letter; attitude of letter writer; meaning of key terms: 'nervous breakdown', 'his mind is still chaos', 'not fit to be trusted with men's lives', 'the public interest'.

Photograph on page 26
Questions to ask
1. Why do you think the soldiers wore metal helmets?
2. Why are there rolls of barbed wire at the top of the trench?
3. What was the worst danger of water-filled trenches?
Points to explore
Background: mud, debris, barbed wire
People: age, gender, clothing, headgear, satchels

Photograph on page 27
Questions to ask
1. The cans being warmed up on this makeshift oven probably contain 'bully beef' – cheap corned beef sent to soldiers on the front line. Why do you think soldiers were sent canned rather than fresh food?
2. Imagine you're a soldier in a World War I trench. Write a letter to a parent describing a typical day.
Points to explore
Background: improvised brick oven, metal lids, cans, earth mound
People: age, gender, clothing, headgear

Picture on page 28
Questions to ask
1. This document records the death of an officer, Wilfred Owen, another famous war poet. Do you think this document should give more information than it does? Why do you think the forms were kept so short?
2. Do some research on Owen, then try writing a letter to his family informing them of his death.
Points to explore
Form: preprinted text (should it ask for more information?); typewritten text (is this enough information to write a letter of condolence?)

Photograph on page 29
Questions to ask
1. How do you think these girls are feeling?
2. What do you think the ropes are for?
Points to explore
Background: open grave, ropes, planks of wood, flowers
People: clothing, ages, expressions

Some suggested answers can be found on the Wayland website www.waylandbooks.co.uk.

Further Information

Books

World War I *(Living Through)* by Nicola Barber (Raintree, 2013)

Voices of World War I *(Voices of War)* by Ann Heinrichs (Capstone, 2010)

The War to End All Wars: World War I by Russell Freedman (Clarion Books, 2010)

Documenting World War I *(Documenting History)* by Philip Steele (Wayland, 2014)

The Usborne Introduction to the First World War by Ruth Brocklehurst and Henry Brook (Usborne, 2007)

Websites

http://www.historylearningsite.co.uk/home_front_1914_to_1918.htm
http://www.bbc.co.uk/history/british/britain_wwone/
http://www.spartacus.schoolnet.co.uk/FWWhome.htm
http://www.nationalarchives.gov.uk/pathways/firstworldwar/spotlights/airraids.htm
http://www.iwm.org.uk/history/rationing-and-food-shortages-during-the-first-world-war

Glossary

allotment A small area of land, rented out by local government or independent associations, to people so they can grow their own food.

amputation an operation to remove a limb that has been damaged by disease or injury.

artillery Large guns used in warfare.

bombardment Continuous attack with bombs, shells or missiles.

civilian A person not in the armed forces.

condolence An expression of sympathy, especially after someone has died.

conscription Compulsory enlistment into the armed forces.

correspondence Written communication.

eligible Having the right to do or become something.

front, the The most advanced position an army has reached – the place where the enemy is or may be engaged.

glamorous Exciting, attractive and special.

hostel A place that provides cheap accomodation for a particular group of people such as students, workers or travellers.

malnutrition Lack of proper nutrition caused by not having enough to eat or not eating enough healthy food.

morale Confidence and enthusiasm.

munitions Military weapons, ammunition and equipment.

next of kin A person's closest living relatives.

rationing A system imposed by governments during times of shortage in which a fixed amount of foods and other essentials is officially allowed to each person.

recruitment The process of enlisting people into the armed forces or other organisations.

refugee A person who has been forced to leave his or her country in order to escape war or some other danger.

Royal Navy The British navy.

shell An explosive artillery projectile.

sulphur A combustible, yellow element.

trenches A connected system of long, narrow ditches used by soldiers on the front line during World War I to protect themselves from enemy fire.

U-boat A German submarine used in World War I and World War II.

voluntary Not compulsory.

war memorial A monument commemorating those killed in a war.

War Office A department of the British government that was in charge of the army between the 17th century and 1964 (when it became part of the Ministry of Defence).

Western Front the front line in France, where the British army spent much of the war fighting.

workhouse A place where the poor were given food and lodging in return for work.

World War I A war in which the Central Powers (Germany, Austria-Hungary, Turkey and Bulgaria) were defeated by an alliance of Britain, France, Russia, Italy, the USA and others.